Fact Finders™

Questions and Answers: Countries

Rwanda

A Question and Answer Book

by Kathleen W. Deady

Consultant:
Dr. Michele D. Wagner
Assistant Professor of African History
University of Minnesota
Minneapolis, Minnesota

Capstone
press

Mankato, Minnesota

Fact Finders is published by Capstone Press,
151 Good Counsel Drive, P.O. Box 669, Mankato, Minnesota 56002.
www.capstonepress.com

Library of Congress Cataloging-in-Publication Data
Deady, Kathleen W.
    Rwanda: a question and answer book / by Kathleen W. Deady
    p. cm.—(Fact finders. Questions and answers. Countries)
    Includes bibliographical references and index.
    ISBN 0-7368-3759-0 (hardcover)
    ISBN 0-7368-5208-5 (paperback)
    1. Rwanda—Juvenile literature. I. Title. II. Series.
DT450.14.D43 2005
967.571—dc22   2004011358

Summary: Describes the geography, history, economy, and culture of Rwanda in a
    question-and-answer format.

Editorial Credits

Katy Kudela, editor; Kia Adams, set designer; Kate Opseth, book designer; Nancy
    Steers, map illustrator; Wanda Winch, photo researcher; Scott Thoms, photo editor

Photo Credits

Art Directors/Howard Sayer, cover (background), 27; Bruce Coleman Inc./A. Van
Zandbergen, cover (foreground), 13; Bruce Coleman Inc./Charles Henneghien, 23;
Bruce Coleman Inc./Peter Davey, 1; Capstone Press, 29 (flag); Corbis/Reuters, 8–9;
Digital Vision/Gerry Ellis and Karl Ammann, 4; Panos Pictures/Giacomo Pirozzi, 17;
Peter Arnold Inc./Das Fotoarchiv/SVT Bild, 7; Photo courtesy of Alison Keroack, 29
(coins); Photo courtesy of Richard Sutherland, 29 (bill); Robert J. Ross, 12, 14–15, 21, 25;
Ronald de Hommel, 11, 19

Artistic Effects

Ingram Publishing, 24; Photodisc/Jules Frazier, 18

1 2 3 4 5 6 10 09 08 07 06 05

Table of Contents

Features

Where is Rwanda?

Rwanda is in east-central Africa. It is slightly smaller than the U.S. state of Maryland.

Mountains cover most of northwest Rwanda. Mountain gorillas make their homes in the forests of some of these mountains.

Mountain gorillas live in the forests of Rwanda. ➤

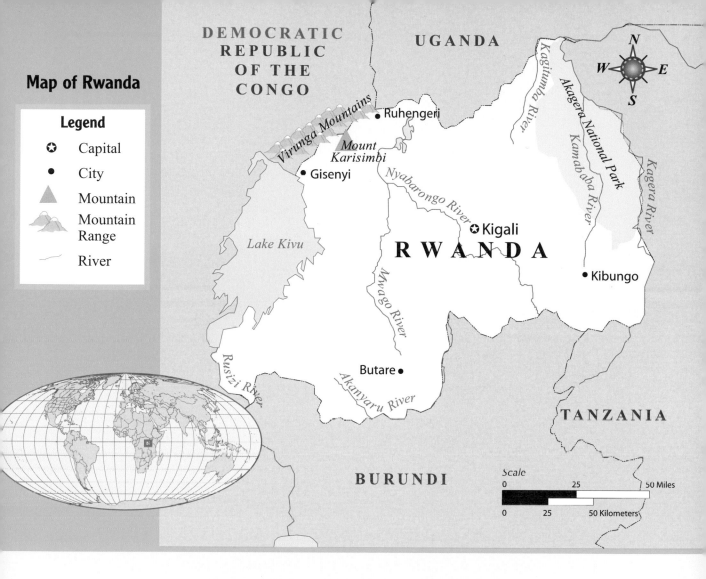

Map of Rwanda

Legend

- ✪ Capital
- ● City
- ▲ Mountain
- ⛰ Mountain Range
- 〜 River

Central Rwanda has rolling hills and marshy valleys. This land is good for farming.

Eastern Rwanda is flat and dry. At Akagera National Park, giraffes, zebras, and other animals graze on the grasslands.

When did Rwanda become a country?

Rwanda became an **independent** country on July 1, 1962. Before that, Belgium ruled the country. Belgium ruled with the help of one of Rwanda's ethnic groups, the **Tutsi**. Rwanda's other ethnic groups were the **Hutu** and the **Twa**.

European explorers first came to Rwanda in the 1890s. In 1923, Belgium took control of Rwanda. To rule the country, the Belgians worked together with the rich and powerful Tutsi. Other Rwandans were not treated as well, especially the Hutu.

Fact!

In 1933, Belgium issued identity cards. People in Rwanda had to carry these cards. A card listed if a person was a Tutsi, a Hutu, or a Twa.

On July 1, 1962, Rwandans gathered to celebrate their independence from Belgium.

In 1959, fights broke out between the Hutu and Tutsi. The Tutsi leaders lost their power. In 1962, Belgium gave up control. For many years, fighting continued in Rwanda.

The Hutu and Tutsi fought a **civil war** in the 1990s. By the war's end in 1994, at least 1 million people had died.

What type of government does Rwanda have?

Rwanda's government is a **republic**. In this type of government, people vote for their leaders. Rwandans age 18 years and older can vote in elections. People vote for national leaders, including the president and members of **parliament**.

Rwanda's president leads the country. The president chooses people to help run the country. This group is called the cabinet.

Fact!

In response to fighting, the Rwandan government passed a new law. Under the law, the government will no longer recognize people as Tutsi, Hutu, or Twa. All people will be called Rwandans.

People in Rwanda line up to vote for government leaders.

Rwanda's parliament makes new laws for the country. Members of this group come from all the regions of Rwanda.

In 2003, the Rwandan government wrote a new constitution. These written laws called for equal treatment for all Rwandans.

What kind of housing does Rwanda have?

Most families live on farms outside cities. A farm usually has several buildings for people and animals. This group of buildings is called a *rugo*. Farms are scattered through Rwanda's many hills. Rwandans usually think of their hill as their community.

Where do people in Rwanda live?

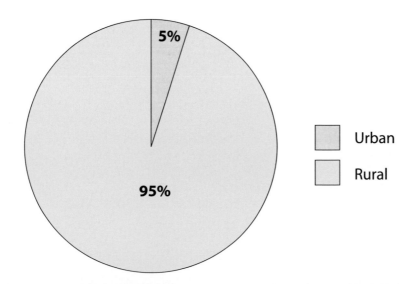

5%

95%

Urban

Rural

Houses are built on hillsides in the capital city of Kigali.

Many homes in Rwanda do not have electricity or water. People must get water from a river or a well.

In the cities, rich Rwandans have modern homes made of brick or concrete. These homes have water and electricity.

What are Rwanda's forms of transportation?

Most Rwandans walk or ride bicycles to get where they need to go. In towns, they ride buses, vans, or taxis. People also ride in vans or minibuses that travel from town to town.

Only a few Rwandans own cars. Those with cars sometimes offer others rides to help them travel longer distances.

Most people in Rwanda walk from place to place. ➤

Rwandans use canoes to travel on rivers and lakes.

Transporting goods, such as food, long distances is a challenge for Rwandans. The country has one main airport but few planes. The country's large boats cannot pass through the shallow rivers. Instead, many Rwandans use canoes on the rivers.

What are Rwanda's major industries?

Agriculture is Rwanda's main industry. Almost all Rwandans are farmers. They grow food for their families. Extra crops are sold at markets or to other countries.

Rwandans grow most of the foods they eat. They grow beans, bananas, and sweet potatoes. They also grow cassava root and sorghum grain. Most families also raise livestock, including goats, cattle, and chickens.

What does Rwanda import and export?

Imports	Exports
cement	animal hides
machinery and equipment	coffee
petroleum products	tea

Farming is a part of life for most Rwandans.

Rwandans grow crops and raise livestock to sell. Coffee is the main cash crop. Animal hides and tea are also sold.

Factories are a smaller industry in Rwanda. Factories make goods to sell, including soft drinks and shoes.

What is school like in Rwanda?

Rwandan children ages 7 to 12 are supposed to go to school. Many children do not. Their families cannot afford to pay for school uniforms and supplies.

Some children attend school for a few years but quit early. Often these children help at home with farm chores.

Fact!

Only 12 in every 100 Rwandan children attend high school. About 7 out of every 1,000 go on to a university.

Some Rwandan children meet for classes outdoors.

The civil war in the 1990s destroyed many school buildings. Many teachers died in the war. Today, the Rwandan government is working to rebuild its schools and to educate more children.

What are Rwanda's favorite sports and games?

The most popular sport in Rwanda is soccer. Children throughout Rwanda play soccer. They make soccer balls from rolled banana leaves, plastic bags, or rags.

Many communities have soccer clubs and teams. People go to local soccer games. Children and adults also listen to national games on the radio.

Rwandans also enjoy other sports. Running, basketball, and volleyball are popular sports.

Fact!

In 1997, people gathered in Rwanda for the first soccer tournament since the civil war. Rwanda beat soccer teams from other countries to win the championship.

Children play soccer with handmade soccer balls.

A popular game with children and adults is *igisoro*. Players use a wooden board with hollowed-out holes. They use 48 seeds or stones for counters. Players move the counters around the board and try to capture them all.

What are the traditional art forms in Rwanda?

Music, dance, and crafts are part of life in Rwanda. Children begin learning songs and dances at a young age. They learn **traditional** and modern dances.

Rwandans play music on both modern and traditional instruments. Some people play the guitar. Others play traditional instruments, like drums.

Fact!

Rwandans enjoy poetry and stories. Storytellers are honored in Rwandan homes. The stories they share often have a message and teach values.

Weaving baskets is a common craft in Rwanda.

Rwanda is known for its crafts. Weavers use sticky banana leaves and grasses to make baskets and mats. Other people make woodcarvings and jewelry. Many artists sell their crafts in the cities.

What major holidays do people in Rwanda celebrate?

Rwandans celebrate some religious holidays. On Christmas, Christian families may go to church and share meals. Other families observe Islamic holidays, such as Ramadan. During this month, **Muslims** do not eat or drink from sunrise to sunset.

Family events are also a time for Rwandans to celebrate. People gather for weddings and other events. Weddings are a time for food, music, and dance.

What other holidays do people in Rwanda celebrate?

Easter
Labor Day
New Year's Day

Music and dance are a part of many holidays.

People take time to remember sad events in Rwanda's history. In early April, Rwandans hold a memorial week. During this week, people remember those who died because of the civil war.

What are the traditional foods of Rwanda?

Rwandans eat what they grow. Beans, bananas, and roasted sweet potatoes are common. Rwandans use sorghum grain to make a thin pudding called porridge.

Nearly everyone eats *ubugali*. Rwandans use corn, sorghum, or cassava flour to make a dough. They dip a ball of this cooked dough in a sauce made from vegetables, beans, or meat.

Fact!

Rwanda has its own type of fast food. People can stop by places along the road to buy roasted corn, meat, peanuts, and hard-boiled eggs.

Rwandans grow many kinds of bananas.

In the capital city of Kigali, people have more foods available. Wealthy Rwandans eat meat often. Goat and beef are most common. Some people who live near water eat fish.

What is family life like in Rwanda?

Close family life has always been important in Rwanda. Before the civil war, families were large. Grandparents, aunts, uncles, and cousins often lived near each other. They saw each other almost every day.

What are the ethnic backgrounds of people in Rwanda?

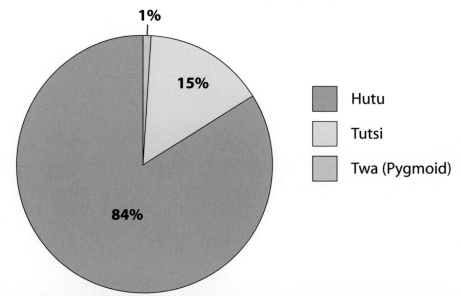

1%

15%

84%

Hutu

Tutsi

Twa (Pygmoid)

Some Rwandan grandparents help take care of children.

Since the war, most families have changed in some way. Many people died in the war, especially men. Many women now support their families. Some children help take care of their families.

Rwanda Fast Facts

Official name:

Rwandese Republic

Land area:

9,632 square miles
(24,947 square kilometers)

Average annual precipitation:

31 inches (79 centimeters)

Average January temperature (Kigali):

67 degrees Fahrenheit
(19 degrees Celsius)

Average July temperature (Kigali):

70 degrees Fahrenheit
(21 degrees Celsius)

Population:

7,954,013 people

Capital city:

Kigali

Languages:

Kinyarwanda, French, and English

Natural resources:

farmland, gold, hydropower, tin ore, tungsten ore

Religions:

Roman Catholic	56%
Protestant	26%
Adventist	11%
Islamic	5%
Other	2%

Money and Flag

Money:

Rwanda's money is called the Rwandan franc (RWF). In 2004, 1 U.S. dollar equaled about 555 RWFs. One Canadian dollar equaled about 419 RWFs.

Flag:

Rwanda's flag has three stripes of blue, yellow, and green. The blue stripe is a symbol of happiness and peace. The yellow stripe stands for wealth. The green stripe is a symbol of hope. In the top right corner is a sun. The sun stands for the light that guides Rwandans.

Learn to Speak Kinyarwanda

Rwandans speak three official languages. These languages are Kinyarwanda, French, and English. Learn to speak some Kinyarwanda using the words below.

English	Kinyarwanda	Pronunciation
good morning	mwaramutseho	(MWAR-uh-moots-AY-ho)
good evening	mwiriweho	(MWEER-ee-WAY-ho)
How are you?	makuru ki	(mah-KOO-roo-key)
I'm well	ni byiza	(nee-BEE-zuh)
thank you	murakoze	(MOO-rah-KO-zay)
yes	yego	(YAY-go)
no	oya	(OH-yah)

Glossary

civil war (SIV-il WOR)—war between groups of people in the same country

Hutu (HOO-too)—the largest ethnic group in Rwanda; all people in Rwanda are now called Rwandans.

independent (in-di-PEN-duhnt)—free from the control of other people or things

Muslim (MUHZ-luhm)—a person who follows the Islamic religion; Islam is based on the teachings of Muhammad.

parliament (PAR-luh-muhnt)—the group of people who have been elected to make laws in some countries

republic (ree-PUHB-lik)—a government headed by a president with officials elected by the people

rugo (ROO-goh)—a traditional group of beehive-shaped homes, with the main home in the middle, and a fence around the group

traditional (tra-DISH-uh-nuhl)—handed down from one generation to the next, such as ideas or beliefs

Tutsi (TOOT-see)—an ethnic group in Rwanda; all people in Rwanda are now called Rwandans.

Twa (TWA)—a small ethnic group in Rwanda; all people in Rwanda are now called Rwandans.

Internet Sites

FactHound offers a safe, fun way to find Internet sites related to this book. All of the sites on FactHound have been researched by our staff.

Here's how:
1. Visit *www.facthound.com*
2. Type in this special code **0736837590** for age-appropriate sites. Or enter a search word related to this book for a more general search.
3. Click on the **Fetch It** button.

FactHound will fetch the best sites for you!

Read More

Fowler, Allan. *Africa.* Rookie Read-About Geography. New York: Children's Press, 2001.

Graf, Mike. *Africa.* Continents. Mankato, Minn.: Bridgestone Books, 2003.

Isaac, John. *Rwanda: Fierce Clashes in Central Africa.* Children in Crisis. Woodbridge, Conn.: Blackbirch Press, 1997.

Index